# The Feeling

By

Dottie Randazzo

# The Feeling

by

Dottie Randazzo

Published by:

Creative Dreaming

6433 Topanga Cyn. Blvd.

Woodland Hills, CA 91303

All rights reserved. No part of this book may be reproduced or transmitted in any form or by any means, electronic or mechanical, including photocopying, recording or by any information storage and retrieval system, without permission from the author, except for the inclusion of brief quotations in a review.

Copyright © 2007 by Dottie Randazzo

ISBN 978-0-6151-6439-7

**By Dottie Randazzo**

Praying 101 for Spiritual Enlightenment
Praying 101 for Men
Praying 101 for Women
Praying 101 for Kids & Teens
Praying 101 for Parents

Once upon a time there lived a girl who wanted more

out of life.

She looked at the world around her and wondered why some people had everything they wanted and others did not.

She had been told

that

"Life was not fair."

She did not believe

that

life was not fair.

She began to read about life.

She read books about positive thinking.

She read books about visualization.

She read books
about believing.

She read books about human nature.

She read books about magic.

She read books about quantum physics.

She read books about the brain and how the mind works.

She read books about praying.

She read books
about affirmations.

She read books about intuition.

She read books about miracles.

She read books about the soul.

She read books about spirituality.

She read books about the mysteries of the universe.

She read books about all the different world religions.

With her new knowledge she began to practice what she had read.

She began praying.

She began

visualizing.

She began thinking positively.

She began saying affirmations.

She did not get what she wanted.

She expanded her search to find out why some people had everything they wanted and others did not.

She took seminars.

She got hypnotized.

She watched movies.

She joined several spiritual organizations.

With all the information she had acquired, the girl still did not know how to get what she wanted.

She began to sit and think about all of the valuable information that she had learned.

She spent an enormous amount of time thinking and thinking and then thinking some more.

What she discovered was that all the praying, affirmations, positive thinking, and visualizing would not get you what you wanted without….

# The Feeling

She remembered that the times she had a feeling about something, were the times that something happened.

She realized that none of what she studied would work without The Feeling.

She began to experiment with The Feeling.

She closed her eyes and conjured up a feeling.

She told herself that she had the feeling it was going to be a fantastic day.

As she said the words, to herself, she felt a tingle go through her body.

A smile came upon her face because she knew it was The Feeling.

She only said it twice and the entire process took merely seconds.

She felt excited upon opening her eyes.

She knew the tingle she felt was her energy going out to the universe to manifest itself.

The day that followed was a fantastic day.

The next morning she decided to experiment with The Feeling again.

She had to go to a public office where the wait times were usually hours.

She closed her eyes and told herself, *"I have the feeling that my wait time at this public place will not be long."*

As she said the words she felt a tingly vibration running through her body.

A smile came across her face because she knew she had The Feeling.

That day she walked in and out of the public office in mere minutes.

She was very excited about her new discovery.

She told her friends who experimented with The Feeling.

They too had astonishing results with mere seconds of time dedicated to The Feeling.

She thought about
the limitations of
The Feeling.

To test The Feeling she closed her eyes and said to herself, "*I have the feeling I will win a million dollars today.*"

She did not get the tingly feeling that she had experienced before.

She said it again in hopes of invoking The Feeling.

She could not get

The Feeling.

She thought and thought and thought some more.

She closed her eyes and said to herself, *"I have The Feeling I know how The Feeling works."*

She felt the tingly feeling of the energy going through her body.

She opened her eyes and instantly knew that we can only invoke The Feeling in accordance with our belief system.

If she did not believe that something could or would occur, she could not, no matter how hard she tried, invoke the tingly feeling throughout her body.

She closed her eyes and thought about a place that she wanted to go and see.

As she thought about the place, she felt the tingly sensation, that she acknowledged as The Feeling, go through her body.

To her amazement,
a few hours later a
friend called her
to extend an invitation
to the very place she
had thought about
while invoking
The Feeling.

Still wanting to be one hundred percent sure about her new discovery, she tried it again.

This time she closed her eyes and thought about a beautiful white unicorn just outside her door.

No matter how vivid the picture was in her mind she could not invoke the tingly sensation throughout her body.

She closed her eyes and tried with all her might to get The Feeling.

The tingly feeling could not and would not happen.

The girl then knew that The Feeling works in conjunction with your belief system.

If you don't believe
it, you won't feel it.

# If you don't feel it, you won't manifest it.

Finally, after all of her searching, the girl knew why some people have everything they want and other people don't.

The girl then realized that her beliefs had a lot to do with what she had and didn't have in her life.

If she didn't believe she could have something or deserved something, she could not get The Feeling.

This got the girl to thinking about all the beliefs she had gathered over her lifetime.

The girl began to think about her beliefs regarding money and possessions.

She changed her beliefs about money, and more money came into her life.

She changed her beliefs about material possessions and was able to obtain whatever her heart desired.

She changed her beliefs about relationships and more loving relationships began entering her life.

The girl knew why some people had everything and others did not.

**I**t was The Feeling

that made the

difference.

The End

www.ingramcontent.com/pod-product-compliance
Lightning Source LLC
Chambersburg PA
CBHW032021040426
42448CB00006B/693